Multi-Colored Human?

ISBN 979-8-89130-132-0 (paperback)
ISBN 979-8-89130-134-4 (digital)

Copyright © 2024 by Mike Kipp

All rights reserved. No part of this publication may be reproduced, distributed, or transmitted in any form or by any means, including photocopying, recording, or other electronic or mechanical methods without the prior written permission of the publisher. For permission requests, solicit the publisher via the address below.

Christian Faith Publishing
832 Park Avenue
Meadville, PA 16335
www.christianfaithpublishing.com

Printed in the United States of America

Multi-Colored Human?

Mike Kipp

I am not just purple
You are not just green
It's not by one color
We wish to be seen

I look in the mirror
And what do I see?
A Multi-Colored Human
Staring back at me

All over our bodies
Various pigments abound
A person of one solid color
No one has ever found

Look closely at your skin,
Eyes, nails, teeth, and hair
I bet you found multiple
Colors lurking there

Stick out your tongue
And move it side to side
That's just one more color
Most of the time, we hide

Sometimes skin changes color
When it's bruised, burnt, or cold
Hair and skin color can change
When people get really old

Please don't call me a color
I'm not purple or green
I'm not even one color
Somewhere in between

You need not look hard
To realize neither are you
You're not just one color
Not even just two

It's easy to see
You're Multi-Colored like me
We're *all* Multi-Colored
Multi-Colored Humans are we

Let's examine how we view
Ourselves and each other
Neither you nor I
Should be defined by a color

About the Author

Mike Kipp has been involved in education for over four decades. As a teacher, coach, and athletic director, Coach Kipp, as he's usually called, has had the opportunity to be involved with students from many different ethnic and economic backgrounds. He's taught and coached in the city, the suburbs, small towns, and at a boarding school with students from all over the world.

    Mike is also a minister. He has served as a leader in children's programs, and in youth, family, and recreation ministry. Coach Mike Kipp now wants to help people, especially children, view others from their unique *sameness*, rather than their differences, when it comes to ethnicity and predominant skin color.